Contents

MYTHOLOGY and LEGENDS around the WORLD

The Myths and Legends of Ancient Greece and Rome

Edited by Joanne Randolph

Cavendish Square
New York

Published in 2018 by Cavendish Square Publishing, LLC
243 5th Avenue, Suite 136, New York, NY 10016

First Edition

Website: cavendishsq.com

Cataloging-in-Publication Data

Names: Randolph, Joanne, editor.
Title: The myths and legends of ancient Greece and Rome / edited by Joanne Randolph.
Description: New York : Cavendish Square Publishing, 2018. | Series: Mythology and legends around the world | Includes glossary and index. | Audience: Grades 3-8.
Identifiers: ISBN 9781502632760 (library bound) | ISBN 9781502634467 (pbk.) | ISBN 9781502633040 (ebook)
Subjects: LCSH: Mythology, Classical--Juvenile literature.
Classification: LCC BL725.R36 2018 | DDC 398.20938--dc23

Editorial Director: David McNamara
Editor: Caitlyn Miller
Copy Editor: Rebecca Rohan
Associate Art Director: Amy Greenan
Designer: Megan Mette
Production Coordinator: Karol Szymczuk
Photo Research: J8 Media

"On to Olympus" by Charles F. Baker from *Calliope* Magazine (November 2012)
"Atalanta and the Calydonian Boar" by Ann Pedtke from *Cricket* Magazine (May 2011)
"A Meeting With the Dead" by Angela Murock Hussein from *Dig* Magazine (September 2015)
"Pluto: Grim Lord of the Underworld" by Robert D. San Souci from *Odyssey* Magazine (October 1994)
"Heracles and the Cattle of Geryon" By Charles F. Baker from *Calliope* Magazine (May 2007)
"Not So Difficult!" by Diana Childress from *Calliope* Magazine (July 2014)
"Divine Punishment" by Anthony Hollingsworth from *Calliope* Magazine (July 2014)
"Arachne Spins Her Web" by Johanna Arnone from *Muse* Magazine (October 2015).

The photographs in this book are used by permission and through the courtesy of: Cover, North Wind Picture Archives/Alamy Stock Photo; p. 4 Alexander Andreyevich Ivanov (1806–1858)/File: Bellerofont otpravljaetsja v pohod protiv Himery.jpg/Wikimedia Commons; p. 7 Yulia Ryabokon/Alamy Stock Vector; p. 9 Artist unknown/Former Durand and Blacas collections, British Museum/File: Bellerophon Chimaera BM D205.jpg/Wikimedia Commons; p. 10 Bettmann/Getty Images; p. 13 Vasarchit, own work/File: Calydon Aetolia 2010.jpg/Wikimedia Commons; p. 20 Yair Haklai, photographer/British Museum/File: Castor and Pollux-Parc de Versailles.jpg/Wikimedia Commons; pp. 22-23 Drawing by Giulio Romano -1546) François Louis Lonsing, engraver (1739 - 1799)/File: Giulio Romano - Meleager et Atalanta.jpg/Wikimedia Commons; pp. 24-25 Rodkarv/Shutterstock.com; p. 26 Chronicle/Alamy Stock Photo; p. 28 Web Gallery of Art/File: Giovanni Battista Tiepolo - Venus Appearing to Aeneas on the Shores of Carthage - WGA22336.jpg/Wikimedia Commons; p. 30 The Yorck Project: 10.000 Meisterwerke der Malerei/Yale Center for British Art/File: Joseph Mallord William Turner 004.jpg/Wikimedia Commons; p. 32 XQGCpNt3tbJiAw at Google Cultural Institute/Photo: Tate, London, 2011/File: Sir Nathaniel Dance-Holland - The Meeting of Dido and Aeneas - Google Art Project.jpg/Wikimedia Commons; p. 33 De Agostini/Biblioteca Ambrosiana/Getty Images; p. 35 University of Toronto Wenceslaus Hollar Digital Collection/File: Wenceslas Hollar - The Greek gods. Pluto.jpg/Wikimedia Commons; pp. 36-37 PHAS/UIG via Getty Images; p. 38 Michel wal, own work/File: Godecharle Hercule.jpg/Wikimedia Commons; p. 40 Luis García (Zaqarbal), 12 March 2006/File: Mosaico Trabajos Hércules (M.A.N. Madrid) 01.jpg/Wikimedia Commons; p. 41 Galería online, Museo del Prado/File: Hércules lucha con la hidra de Lerna, por Zurbarán.jpg/Wikimedia Commons; p. 43 DEA/L. Pedicini/Getty Images; p. 45 Los Angeles County Museum of Art/File: Hercules and the Bull of Poseidon LACMA 65.37.13.jpg/Wikimedia Commons; p. 47 DEA/G. Dagli Orti/Getty Images; p. 48 Rolf Krahl (Rotkraut), own work/File: Barockgarten Großsedlitz - Hera.jpg/Wikimedia Commons; pp. 50-51 unknown photographer/File: Botticelli-Juicio-de-Paris.jpg/Wikimedia Commons; pp. 54-55 De Agostini Picture Library/Getty Images; p. 57 Vincent de Groot , own work/File: Spider vdg.jpg/Wikimedia Commons; p. 58 [1] (http://artyzm.com/obrazy/veronese_arachne.jpg)/File: Veronese, Paolo - Arachne or Dialectics - 1520.jpg/Wikimedia Commons.

Printed in the United States of America

1

Greek and Roman Myths and Legends

Throughout history, people have created bodies of stories to explain natural **phenomena**, the beginnings of life on Earth, life and death, religion, and many other themes that confused or frightened them or seemed to have no explanation. These stories are called **myths**.

At first, these myths and stories were told out loud, and that is how they were passed on. Over time, the stories changed slightly. Around the eighth century BCE, a poet called Homer wrote down the Greek myths. Because of this written record, these stories were preserved, and we can study them today.

There is a lot of overlap between Greek and Roman myths. Many of the stories are the same, but the gods, goddesses, and heroes have different names. For example,

Opposite: This painting depicts Bellerophon with the flying stallion, Pegasus. Bellerophon and Pegasus were sent on many heroic quests.

the Greek ruler of the gods is Zeus, while the Roman name for this god is Jupiter. The famed hero Hercules in Roman stories is named Heracles in Greek stories. In the following pages, we will take a look at some well-known Greek and Roman myths and **legends**.

On to Olympus

Have you ever heard a tale that tells of a hero who rides in pursuit of a horrible dragon, slays it, and then returns to marry the king's daughter? There are actually many such tales, including one that the Greeks told about a prince named Bellerophon.

After Bellerophon accidentally killed a man, he sought a difficult task as a way of atoning for his crime. Bellerophon was the son of the king of Corinth, a well-known and powerful **city-state** in central Greece, and he knew he had to make amends. He soon left Corinth and traveled to the neighboring city-state of Argos. There he asked King Proetus to assign him a task. Unfortunately, when Proetus's wife saw the young prince, she fell in love with him. Bellerophon, however, did not return the feeling. Furious at the rejection, the queen falsely accused Bellerophon of improper conduct. What was the king to do? **Custom** dictated that one did not harm a guest! After

This image shows some of the main Greek gods. Many of these gods have a counterpart in Roman mythology.

much thought, Proetus sent Bellerophon to his father-in-law, the king of Lycia in Asia Minor (present-day Turkey), with a letter that read, "This man has committed a very serious crime. Kill him."

Kill a Guest—No Way!

Unaware of the contents of the letter, Bellerophon left for Lycia. For some nine days, the letter remained unopened. When the king finally did read it, he was shocked. Should he, could he, kill a guest? Definitely not! How would the gods judge him? A better idea was to send Bellerophon on an extremely dangerous mission! And so he did.

For a long time, a horrible, fire-breathing monster had been destroying the lands of Lycia. The creature, called the Chimera, had the body of a lion, the tail of a serpent, and the head of a goat in the middle of its back. Killing this beast was the task the king assigned to Bellerophon.

Meet Pegasus

As was customary when faced with such a dangerous task, Bellerophon sought advice. The wise man he approached told him that he needed the help of the winged horse named Pegasus. The wise man also said that Pegasus was **immortal** and untamed. Bellerophon knew that the goddess Athena had given Pegasus to the Muses as a companion, so he decided to ask her for help.

When Bellerophon awoke the next morning, beside him lay a beautiful golden bridle. After thanking Athena for her gift, Bellerophon went in search of Pegasus. He found him drinking the cool, refreshing waters of the Pierene, a spring in Corinth that was sacred to the Muses. Seeing the golden bridle and knowing that the goddess Athena approved of the mission, Pegasus allowed Bellerophon to mount him, and off they flew to Lycia.

Dreadful to Behold!

Once in Lycia, they saw the dreadful Chimera breathing fire as he roamed the countryside. Bellerophon readied his arrows. Urging Pegasus to swoop low to the ground, Bellerophon quickly killed the fearsome creature. The king then assigned other tasks of equal difficulty. But Bellerophon completed them all. Convinced that the gods were protecting Bellerophon, the king gave him half his kingdom and his daughter in marriage.

In time, Bellerophon began to consider himself equal to the gods. One day, he decided to visit Mount Olympus. He mounted

Bellerophon, riding winged Pegasus, strikes the goat's head on the back of the Chimera with his spear.

This illustration shows Bellerophon struggling to keep control of Pegasus before falling to earth. For the ancient Greeks, this story illustrated the consequences that befell humans who became too proud.

Pegasus, and up they flew. The gods, however, were watching and sent a horsefly to bite Pegasus. Pegasus reared, for he, too, knew that Bellerophon had overstepped his bounds. As a result of the fall that followed, Bellerophon was blinded and crippled. Pegasus, however, continued his flight to Mount Olympus.

2 Atalanta and the Calydonian Boar

Several Greek myths feature a powerful female warrior named Atalanta. Atalanta was well known for her speed. In fact, she lost only one footrace, and that was because her opponent tricked her. Atalanta is most celebrated for her role in the myth of the Calydonian boar. A group of famous hunters pursued the boar. But would they be able to kill their prey?

The Hunt Begins

Atalanta paused on the hillside and gazed down at the city of Calydon, its white walls shining on the banks of the river. She was not especially fond of cities. She much preferred hunting in the wooded hills, her tunic kilted around her knees, her ivory **quiver** slung over her shoulder. This pile of stones hardly seemed worth the long journey from Arcadia, leaving behind the shepherd family who had taken her in as a foundling and raised her as their own. But this kingdom of Calydon needed the aid of a great hunter, and Atalanta doubted that the **posse** of arrogant heroes and princes who always responded to such proclamations would be up to the task.

Although it was harvest time, the fields surrounding the city were empty. Ripened grain rotted on the stalk; grapes grew soft on the vine; the olives withered on the trees. If the people did not soon gather their crops, the entire year's harvest would be lost, and **famine** would follow.

Atalanta knew why the people of Calydon did not dare to venture outside the city walls. The story had traveled all through Greece, even to Atalanta's secluded home in Arcadia. Last year, the Calydonians had reaped such a bountiful harvest that King Oeneus decreed an elaborate thanksgiving celebration. To the altar of Demeter, the goddess of crops, the Calydonians brought the first shafts of grain. To Dionysus, the god of wine, they gave their first harvest of grapes. To Athena, the goddess who bestowed the olive tree upon Greece, they offered the first olives from their orchards. Many other divinities were honored, but in the festivities of joy over the rich harvest, Artemis, the goddess of the hunt, was forgotten.

This photograph shows the ruins of a temple in Calydon.

"There are other powers worth having besides the ability to grow a stalk of barley," the neglected goddess fumed. "We shall see how their fields prosper when they are ravaged by a creature that only a glorious hunter can **vanquish**!"

And so the following year, just as the harvest was ready to be gathered, Artemis sent a monstrous boar to terrorize the kingdom of Calydon. The creature's hide was so tough that no hunter's spear had been able to pierce it. The bristles along the boar's back stood as stiff as the crest of a warrior's helmet, its long tusks curved sharp and menacing, and its eyes flashed like lightning. The boar trampled crops and destroyed vineyards, snapped the boughs from olive trees, and attacked peaceful herds that ranged on the slopes. The people retreated fearfully into the city and barred the gates, looking on helplessly as their crops withered in the fields.

No Fear

Atalanta doubted some of the incredible stories she had heard about the boar, but when the proclamation went out calling for great heroes to come to the city's aid, she set off for Calydon. Her **expeditions** in the familiar woods of Arcadia had grown too tame, and she was eager to win fame and honor like that of the mythical heroes.

Now that she was here, looking down upon the empty fields, Atalanta began to think that some of the tales of the boar's ferocity might be true. Well, no matter. She had grown up in the forest, her aim with a bow and arrow was sure, and she knew that the most important skill of a huntress was patience—a quality that the other heroes on the quest were likely to lack. She would hunt the beast down, then return to the friendly green hills of Arcadia, taking with her the reputation of a great huntress. She adjusted the quiver on her shoulder, picked up her bow, and headed down the hill to the city.

Don't Doubt Atalanta

Atalanta was not the first to arrive at Calydon. When she reached the city, a wide assortment of heroes were already polishing their spears outside the gates.

"What are you doing here, girl?" one warrior demanded.

"I am here to hunt the Calydonian boar," Atalanta informed him. "And after *my* arrow brings the creature down, I will take his tusks home with me as a trophy."

There was a collective guffaw from the heroes, and the man who had questioned Atalanta abruptly threw down his spear and stepped close to her. "This is serious business," he growled.

"King Oeneus and Prince Meleager have gathered the greatest heroes in Greece to hunt this boar. Some of us have battled monsters that you can't even imagine. We've fought wars and sacked cities. We're not going to have some girl tagging along on this hunt."

"If you do win the tusks," came a calmer voice from behind him, "how are you going to carry them home on those slender shoulders?" The crowd of men parted with a murmur, and a young man sitting against the stone wall stood up to face Atalanta. "I'd hate to see that pretty face scratched up by briars on the hunt," he added, a grin playing at the corners of his mouth.

Atalanta glowered. "I grew up fighting off bears and wolves to protect our flocks," she said. "I could certainly carry the tusks home with me—*after* I had killed the boar!"

"Prince Meleager, she's just a girl. Send her away so we can—"

"Don't tell me you're afraid to match your spear against this pretty girl's arrows, Telamon?" The smile that had been playing on the young man's lips broke into a full, mocking grin. So this was Calydon's prince, Atalanta thought. Just like the rest of them. Handsome face, strapping muscles, and enough pride to swallow him whole.

"Who's afraid to let this girl join the hunt?" Meleager asked, turning to face each of the heroes in turn. "Theseus? Jason? Nestor? Anyone? ... No? All right, then." He turned back to Atalanta. "It's settled."

And They All Boasted

On the morning of the hunt, Atalanta greased her bowstring while the other heroes argued over who would win the glory of slaying the boar.

"I fought in the great battle against the centaurs, and centaurs are far fiercer than any boar," claimed Nestor.

"That's nothing. I killed the Minotaur himself," boasted Theseus. "Can you imagine the danger of making your way through a labyrinth deep in a castle's dungeons, never knowing when an enormous man-eating bull might leap out at you?"

Jason snorted in derision. "It's all very easy when the task is set before you so simply. Try sailing to the edge of the world to find a Golden Fleece you've never even seen."

"That sort of fame is well enough," retorted Castor and Pollux as they swung themselves haughtily onto their snowy white horses. "But we are sons of the great god Zeus himself. He has helped us to win fame all across Greece for our horsemanship, and he certainly won't fail us in a simple thing like this."

"I challenge any of you to compare your fancy pedigrees to *this.*" Telamon held up his arm to display the bulging muscle. "Any spear I throw will hit home. I don't have to resort to standing at a safe distance and peppering my prey with arrows like a girl." He threw a contemptuous glance at Atalanta, but she simply continued greasing her bowstring. All heroes were the same. What did other girls want with husbands if they were all braggarts like these? Much better to be a huntress and fend for herself.

Atalanta Makes Her Mark

The hunting party set off. Soon enough, the rolling fields in the river valley fell away, and the group entered a forest of trees so immense that Atalanta knew no ax had ever touched them. Telamon, walking in front with Meleager, soon came across the boar's tracks in the soft forest floor. Atalanta bent to spread her hand over one of the muddy prints and marveled at the size. Could the boar be as immense as the stories told? She felt at home in the green gloom of the woods, though, so she straightened and continued on boldly, keeping her ears attuned to every small sound that the forest offered. After some time, they came to a marshy hollow, where bulrushes and swamp grass sprouted. No birds or insects hummed over the damp ground, and Atalanta caught a strange, sharp scent that she couldn't recognize.

"Are you sure you don't want to go back?" Meleager was beside her, distractedly grinding the tip of his spear into the ground. "You've shown your honor in standing up to Telamon, but there's no need for you to come any farther. You've seen the prints now—you know that there's some truth to all the stories. However good you may be at keeping the wolves away from your flocks, you can't kill this thing. Best to leave it to us." He smiled. "Having those big tusks to hang on your wall isn't worth it."

Atalanta shook her head. "If I'm so helpless, why don't you just ..."

At that moment, the forest was split with an enormous crash as the boar came charging toward them. Meleager and Atalanta dodged to each side as the creature hurtled past between them. The boar was as large as a horse, with tusks like spears. Atalanta could feel its hot breath as it rushed by.

Obstacles Arise

"He's mine!" shouted one hero. "I've got a clear shot!" shouted another. But their spears collided in midair, and the boar charged on. The beast tore through the trees, leveling his deadly tusks at first one man, then another. Atalanta collected her wits and readied an arrow, taking care not to catch the boar's attention until he came just within range. She knew that, despite the full quiver of arrows at her back, she must wait for the one shot

The twin brothers, Castor and Pollux

that would make a difference. That was the only way to conquer a beast so fearsome without goading it to fury. Telamon and the other men could show her brute strength. She would show them patience.

Jason let fly his great shaft, but it glanced off the boar's broad back without slowing the creature's pace. Stunned, Jason stumbled back into Nestor as the boar turned to face its attacker. Jason dodged, and Nestor used his long lance to vault into the crotch of an oak. He scrambled to higher branches as the boar gnashed its great tusks against the trunk.

"Clear the way!" Castor and Pollux galloped forward on their white horses, brandishing their spears. Just as they were about to launch their shafts, the boar dove into the low brush. Shouting in dismay at their inability to follow, the brothers reared back their mounts.

Telamon tightened his grip on his spear. "You fools would let it get away!" he cried, and he ducked under the overhanging branches in close pursuit. But the next moment, a jutting root sent him sprawling on the ground, his spear rolling away under the brush. The boar snorted and turned back to charge the fallen man.

Atalanta saw her shot. There was no longer any question of glory, only the fact that one of her fellow huntsmen was about to be trampled and she could halt the stampeding animal in its tracks. The arrow was already nocked in her bow. She drew the string back and let it sail. The arrow grazed the top of the boar's back, lodging just beneath its bristly ear.

Success!

The boar staggered. The other heroes rushed to help Telamon to his feet, then Meleager was plunging his

Atalanta has just released her arrow into the boar in this illustration. She is on the far left, and Meleager is to her right sticking his spear into the boar.

spear between the boar's shoulders, and it was over. The massive beast lay dead on the ground. The men stood back, as if almost afraid to touch the monster. Instead, they focused their attention on Meleager, shaking his hand and offering congratulations, remarking how fitting it was that Calydon's own prince should be the one to vanquish the boar.

Atalanta stood forgotten at the edge of the group. She could only gaze at the boar. The creature was every inch as big as the stories had related, and for a moment its eyes had indeed seemed to flash like lightning. No animal had truly frightened her before. But this beast, sent by a wrathful goddess, had earned her fear.

And her respect.

She had been the one to halt the boar, to save Telamon's life. She knew that Telamon would never acknowledge the debt, nor would the other men recognize her share of the glory. But it didn't matter. She had been patient enough to await her chance, and she had saved the kingdom of Calydon from famine. She had proven herself a great huntress.

"Wait!" It was Meleager's voice, calling out from the center of the crowd of hunters. "Atalanta's arrow drew first blood, and it was Atalanta who made the boar stumble so that I could cast my spear." His eyes met hers, and the smile on his lips was not mocking but full of regard. "Atalanta will share the trophies and the glory of this victory!"

"Prince," began Castor, "if you wish to give the trophies away, by rights they should go to ..."

"By rights they should go to her." Meleager's gaze was steady as he faced the circle of heroes. "You have all done spectacular deeds, and I thank you for your help to my kingdom. But today, the prize goes to one who knows that spectacular deeds sometimes require coolheaded patience." He turned back to Atalanta and gestured at the boar's gleaming tusks. "They're yours," he said. "Perhaps," he added, "you could bring them back to the city and share in our celebrations?"

Atalanta thought of her green hills in Arcadia, and then of how the sun shone on the river as it wound past Calydon. A coolheaded huntress always weighed her options carefully, rather than coming to hasty conclusions. Maybe even an arrogant prince could be worth getting to know a little better. Atalanta would stay in Calydon for a while and see.

This photograph shows the idyllic landscape of Arcadia.

3 The Hero Aeneas

Aeneas was featured in both Greek and Roman myths and legends. In Greek stories, he was a hero of the Trojan War and son to Prince Anchises and the goddess Aphrodite (Venus in Roman mythology). In Roman stories, he is a descendant of Romulus and Remus, the brothers raised by wolves and the founders of Rome. He was the main character in many stories, but we will focus on one that brought him to a very dark and dangerous place.

A Meeting with the Dead

A difficult journey had brought Aeneas to Italy. Once there, however, he learned that he would have to make an even more difficult journey to secure a home for his people. Who could help him do this? Aeneas knew the answer—the dead in the **Underworld**. According

Opposite: In this engraving, the hero Aeneas has found the golden bough that will give him access to a place called the Underworld.

to ancient Roman belief, humans cannot do anything without the gods' favor, and the only way to find out secret information about what was to happen was to ask the dead, since they could see the past and the future.

Definitely Not the First

Aeneas asked Deiphobe, the sibyl of Cumae, for help with this difficult journey. The dead, according to the ancient Greeks and Romans, all went to the same place when they died. Referred to as the Underworld, because it was under the ground, it was well guarded. Only the dead and those with special knowledge or extraordinary powers could enter. For example, the Greek hero Orpheus visited the Underworld and was able to soothe the fearsome creatures there with his extraordinary singing. Odysseus, who fought

Aeneas was said to be the son of Aphrodite, or Venus. In this painting, Aphrodite appears above Aeneas on the shores of Carthage.

against Aeneas at Troy, entered with advice from the sorceress Circe.

But First, You Must ...

Deiphobe agreed to show Aeneas how to enter and leave the Underworld safely, but first, she said, he had to bury a dead friend. The belief at the time was that, if bodies were left unburied, their souls could not enter the Underworld to find peace. Deiphobe also told Aeneas that he had to find a golden bough, a magical tree branch, in the deepest part of the forest. That bough would be his gift to Proserpine, the queen of the Underworld. Deiphobe said that only a person who destiny decreed could have access to a branch would be able to break it off the tree.

Aeneas found the body of his good friend Misenus on the seashore. Misenus had bragged that he was better at trumpeting on a conch shell than the sea god Triton. For this insult, he was hit with a wave and smashed against the rocks on the beach. Aeneas arranged for Misenus to be cremated and buried. After the funeral, Aeneas asked the gods to send him a sign that he had done well. Two doves, birds sacred to his mother, Venus, flew above him. Aeneas followed the doves, and they led him to the golden

Aeneas and the sybil stand on the shore of Lake Avernus, which according to Roman myth was the entrance to the Underworld.

bough. With the chores assigned by Deiphobe completed, Aeneas was ready.

Before setting off, Aeneas sacrificed black steers to Pluto, the ruler of the Underworld. Aeneas then accompanied the sibyl to the entrance to the Underworld, a rock cavern that went deep underground.

So Many Souls

Eventually, the two reached Acheron, one of the rivers that flowed through the Underworld. There, Aeneas saw restless souls waiting on the bank of the river. These souls belonged to people who had not been buried properly and therefore had to wait 100 years before they would be allowed to cross to the other side. Aeneas recognized his friend Palinurus, who had been swept overboard in a storm. Palinurus had swum to shore but had been killed by hostile locals. The sibyl promised Palinurus that a plague would descend on those who had killed him and that they would build a tomb for him in order to lift the curse.

Then Aeneas saw the ferryman Charon, arriving in his boat to bring the dead to their destination. He would only take the souls who had money for payment—it was the custom for people to be buried with a coin. Charon never took money from the living. Deiphobe showed Charon the golden bough to prove that Aeneas was allowed to enter.

On the Way to the Palace

The realm of the dead was divided, with the souls separated into sections based on how they had died. The most innocent were in the outermost areas. There, Aeneas saw the souls of deceased infants and those who were executed for crimes they did not commit. In the next area were those who had committed suicide. Among them was Dido, who had committed suicide when Aeneas, whom she loved, was forced by the gods to leave her. Saddened to discover her there, he tried to ease her pain by telling her that his departure was not his choice and that he had to go because the gods had demanded it. Dido found no comfort in his words and fled into the shadows.

Dido (*left*) was the founder and first queen of Carthage, which is modern-day Tunisia.

Then, Aeneas came to the area reserved for men who had died in battle. He met his brother-in-law Deiphobus, who had fought alongside him at Troy. His soul was mutilated, as his body had been during the sack of Troy. Deiphobus informed them of the paths ahead. The left would take them to Tartarus, the netherworld of eternal punishment for the souls of those who had committed the most horrible crimes. The right would bring them to Elysium, the realm of the blessed.

The palace of the king and queen of the Underworld was at the entrance to Elysium, and it was at their door that Aeneas left the golden bough. Elysium was a paradise for those who were close to the gods, not necessarily those who had been the least sinful in life. In a fertile green valley there, Aeneas found his father, Anchises.

The River of Forgetfulness

In the distance was a river with souls buzzing over it like bees. Anchises told Aeneas that it was the River Lethe. The souls who drank from its waters forgot their former lives and were now waiting to be born again, their futures already fated. He pointed out to his son some of the souls who would become his descendants, thus answering Aeneas's question about whether he would find a home in Italy. There was Silvius, Aeneas's future son by an Italian wife; Romulus, the descendant of Aeneas's son Ascanius and founder

This engraving from Dante's *Divine Comedy* shows the River Lethe.

of the city of Rome; Julius Caesar, who would become a god after he died; and Augustus Caesar, the first ruler of the Roman Empire. Anchises then led Aeneas and Deiphobe to the Gates of Sleep, through which they returned to the land of the living. Aware that a great future awaited him and his family, Aeneas could now begin to feel some joy.

Pluto: Grim Lord of the Underworld

No visit to the Underworld would be complete without taking a look at Pluto, or Hades, as he was called by the Greeks. Pluto was the god who ruled the dismal kingdom of the dead, which the ancients believed lay underneath the earth.

One well-known myth tells how Pluto longed to find a bride. But no woman wanted to dwell in his joyless kingdom as queen of the dead. Then Pluto fell in love with Proserpine (in Greek, Persephone), the beautiful daughter of Ceres, the goddess of agriculture, fertility, and marriage. With the blessing of his brother Jupiter, Pluto plotted to make Proserpine his queen.

While gathering flowers one day, the maiden Proserpine was lured to a lonely valley by the sight of magical blossoms. There, to her horror, the ground split

Pluto and Proserpine, or Persephone, are shown in the background of this image. The three Furies and Cerberus are shown in the foreground.

open and Pluto, the grim lord of the Underworld, burst forth in a golden chariot drawn by four black horses. Pluto seized her and carried her below, as the ground closed over them.

When Ceres learned what had happened to her daughter, she found herself helpless against Pluto and Jupiter. In despair, she abandoned her duties as goddess of fruitfulness, and the Earth turned barren. A terrible famine resulted. When Jupiter asked Ceres to resume her

duties, the goddess replied that she would let nothing grow until her daughter was returned to her. Jupiter ordered Pluto to return Proserpine.

During her stay in the Underworld, Proserpine refused to eat or drink. But before she left, crafty Pluto begged her to share a meal with him. She took a single pomegranate and ate only six small, sweet seeds. Yet Pluto knew that whoever ate the food of the dead could never return to the land of the living. It was a law that even mighty Jupiter could not change.

Ceres pleaded that the tiny seeds were not enough to condemn her daughter forever to the Underworld. Jupiter decreed that Proserpine must stay with Pluto

This panel from a Roman sarcophagus shows Hades abducting Persephone.

six months a year—one month for each seed. So half the year, Ceres mourns her absent child. These are the months of autumn and winter, when the Earth turns cold and nothing grows. But each spring, the goddess rejoices at her daughter's return, and the Earth becomes fruitful again.

4 Meet Heracles

According to ancient Greek legend, there was once born a demigod (part man and part god) named Heracles (Hercules in Roman myths). His mother, Alcmena, was a human, and his father, Zeus, was the king of the gods. Zeus's wife, the jealous Hera, became incensed when she learned that her husband loved a human, and she hated Alcmena's son, Heracles. Some say that Hera brought about a fit of madness within the half-human Heracles that caused him to perform some horrendous crimes.

Heracles Visits the Oracle

Heracles felt much guilt for his actions and wanted to repent for his crimes. When he was grown, he sought the advice of the **oracle** of Delphi, a priestess who gave messages from the god Apollo to humans. Heracles wanted

Opposite: Hercules, or Heracles, is perhaps one of the most famous figures from Greek and Roman myth. His name has become synonymous with strength.

This Roman mosaic, from around 200 to 250 CE, shows Hercules wrestling the Nemean lion.

to know how he could escape from his dark fate and thus become immortal and free of any curses. His desire was to become a benefactor to all humanity, not a slave to his mortality. The oracle told him to serve the king of Tiryns, Eurystheus, for twelve years. Eurystheus, with Hera's intervention, gave Heracles ten labors he must complete. In the end, Heracles had to perform twelve labors because Eurystheus would not count two of the tasks he completed because he had help.

Not So Difficult!

None of Heracles's labors were easy. However, in comparison with his major accomplishments, such as slaying the Nemean lion as his first task, some have been called "not so difficult." See what you think of these seven "lesser" tasks.

Here Heracles is fighting the hydra, which had multiple heads.

The second labor Eurystheus assigned Heracles was to kill the Hydra of Lernea. This multiheaded water serpent lived in a vast swamp and had the challenging trait of growing two heads for each one that was cut off. How could Heracles even stand securely in the gooey slime with her long scaly body coiled around his legs? But Heracles did stand firm—even after Hera sent a monster crab to pinch his feet. First, he killed the crab. Then, he had his nephew Iolaos bring flaming torches to sear each of the Hydra's necks as he lopped off a head. This clever trick kept new heads from sprouting. One source says that the last head struck off was immortal and that Heracles buried it under a huge boulder.

Capturing the Hind of Ceryneia was the third task. It might have been a less difficult job had it just been a matter of killing her with an arrow. But this female deer with golden antlers was sacred to Artemis, the goddess of the hunt, and Heracles did not wish to offend Artemis. A swift runner, the deer was almost impossible to find. Heracles spent a year tracking her down in the rocky mountainous wilderness of Arcadia, where she lived. According to one account, he finally caught her by pinning her forelegs with an arrow as she swam across the River Ladon toward the Underworld. Then, he loaded her on his shoulders and delivered her to Eurystheus.

Heracles's fourth labor resembled the third, only this time the live animal that Eurystheus ordered captured was a fierce boar. After finding its lair on Mount Erymanthos, Heracles shouted to draw the beast out. As it charged forth, it went straight into a deep snowdrift. Using a stout net, Heracles hauled the struggling animal

This piece of art from the first century BCE shows Heracles killing the Erymanthian boar.

out of the snow and carried it to Mycenae. Eurystheus was so terrified of the beast that he jumped into the bronze storage jar he used as a kind of bomb shelter in times of danger. Ancient artists loved illustrating this labor with Eurystheus peeking out of his hiding place at the mighty Heracles, who has the boar raised, snout down, as though he is about to ram it into the jar.

Heracles's sixth task required him rid Lake Stymphalia of an enormous flock of birds. Some sources said the birds could shoot their feathers like arrows. Another claimed that the winged creatures attacked and ate people. To find the birds, Heracles crossed the dense Arcadian forest to a hill overlooking the lake. He created a great noise with a bronze rattle, which, according to some authors, the goddess Athena had given him. Others, however, say that he made the noise himself. As the frightened birds rose squawking into the air, Heracles shot and killed hundreds. His weapon varies from tale to tale—arrows, hunting sticks, even a slingshot. The birds that managed to escape flew off to a distant island in the Black Sea and never returned to Greece.

Going Farther Afield

Heracles's first six labors took place on the Peloponnesus Peninsula in southern Greece. After that, Eurystheus began sending Heracles farther afield. For the seventh labor, he ordered Heracles to fetch a bull that was terrorizing Crete. Minos, a king on the island, had found the animal washed ashore and promised to sacrifice it to the sea god Poseidon. But the bull was so beautiful that he reneged on his vow. In revenge, Poseidon made the bull wildly ferocious. How, then, did Heracles catch the bull?

Heracles grabs Poseidon's bull by the horns and wrestles it to the ground.

In one telling, he climbed a tree and leaped down onto the bull's back as it passed underneath. In another, he grabbed the bull by the horns with his bare hands and wrestled it to the ground. After subduing the beast, Heracles rode it across land and sea back to Mycenae.

For the eighth labor, Eurystheus sent Heracles north to Thrace to seize four man-eating horses that belonged to King Diomedes. These fierce animals were kept chained to bronze feeding troughs and nourished on the flesh of strangers who passed nearby. Heracles hit Diomedes on the head with his club and tossed him to the ravenous beasts. So distasteful was this meal that the horses lost their appetite for human flesh. Heracles then hitched the now-tame horses to Diomedes's war chariot and drove them to Mycenae.

The Last of the "Easy" Tasks

The last of the "not so difficult" labors was to fetch the golden belt of Hippolyte, queen of the **Amazons**. Eurystheus's daughter Admete wanted this particular accessory for herself. To reach Amazonia, Heracles sailed east into the Black Sea. The warlike queen presented no problem at all, as she fell immediately in love with Heracles. When he explained why he had come, she quickly replied, "Belt? Of course, it's yours! Anything you ask!" Hera was incensed. Disguising herself as an Amazon, she spread rumors that Heracles was going to carry the queen off to Greece. Angry Amazons rose up against Heracles and his shipmates. Suspecting a plot, Heracles killed the queen and seized the belt. After defeating the Amazons in battle, he sailed home, fulfilling his mission, but perhaps losing part of his heart.

This detail from a Roman temple in Sicily, Italy, shows Heracles with the Amazons.

5

Divine Punishment

Heracles was not the only hero whom Hera pursued with a vengeance. There were, in fact, no fewer than four other heroes who felt her wrath. Pelias, the uncle of Jason, had angered Hera when he murdered his stepgrandmother for her cruelty. But it was not his killing of the old woman that incurred the goddess's wrath. Rather, what sparked the divine hatred was Pelias committing the crime in one of Hera's temples.

The Fated Men

Tiresias was another, lesser-known hero who felt Hera's sting. When he was a young man, she changed him into a woman. Later, when he was changed back, he told Zeus that being a man was better than being a woman. That comment was enough to send Hera into a rage. She found Tiresias and struck him blind! Zeus tried to cure him

Opposite: Hera is often depicted with a peacock, which was her sacred animal. Hera was the queen of the gods, and married to Zeus. In Roman mythology, she is called Juno.

but could not. So, he chose to give Tiresias the power of prophecy. Zeus reasoned that, if Tiresias could not see the present world, he would let him see the future world.

The Trojan prince Paris also needs to be added to Hera's hate list. Hera never forgave him for choosing Aphrodite over her as the prettiest goddess. When a golden apple inscribed with the words "to the fairest" was thrown into the wedding celebration of the

Paris presents Aphrodite with the golden apple, choosing her as the fairest of the three goddesses who had tried to claim it.

goddess Thetis, three goddesses—Hera, Aphrodite, and Athena—had each claimed the apple. To settle the disagreement, the three had turned to Zeus for judgment. "Dear Zeus," they said, "who is the fairest?" Zeus, of course, was no fool, and he immediately turned to a mortal to judge. His choice was Paris. Aware that, regardless of his choice, two goddesses would hate him, Paris chose Aphrodite. Hera's hatred of him, and of the Trojans in general, was immediate and led to the Trojan War, a Greek victory, and the destruction of the city of Troy.

After Heracles, the most famous hero to be hunted down by an angry Hera was, without doubt, Aeneas, whom the Romans credited as their founder. Hera, or

Juno, as the Romans called her, detested Aeneas almost as much as she hated Heracles. Not only was he related to the Trojans and a cousin to Paris, but he also carried inside him the bloodline that would someday destroy the city of Carthage. This city was Hera's favorite, and the thought of its destruction made her seethe with anger. Carthage was supposed to be a global power and the ruler of the world, but Aeneas and his descendants were destined to change that.

At first, Hera tried to trick Aeneas into staying in Carthage. She even crafted a marriage between him and Dido, the queen of Carthage. But Aeneas knew he had to leave, and, try as she might, Hera could not destroy him or prevent his fate. Aeneas did reach Italy finally, and the Romans eventually did destroy Carthage.

The Unfortunate Women

Hera's rage, however, was not directed just against men. Several women, including some goddesses, found themselves the target of her anger. Often these females had had children with Zeus, and it was these women especially who experienced the full force of the goddess's fury. Leto, for example, was the mother of the twin deities

Artemis and Apollo. Hera was so upset that Zeus was the father of these future mighty gods that she forced Leto to wander the earth, unable to find a place where she could give birth. When Leto arrived at Delos, the god of the island took pity on her and let her give birth there to the twins.

Semele suffered the worst fate of all. After Hera learned that Zeus had fallen in love with this princess of Thebes, she visited Semele, disguised as an old woman. "Ask Zeus to reveal himself to you in his immortal form, to prove he really is divine," Hera told Semele. In all innocence, Semele followed the old woman's advice. But, when Zeus revealed himself in his divine form, the aura was too much for a mortal to endure, and the princess was burned to ashes. When the tragedy happened, Semele was already pregnant with Zeus's child, so Zeus took the unborn child and sewed it into his thigh. Several months later, he gave birth to the god Dionysus—a happy ending for Zeus, but not so happy for Semele.

Io, too, suffered the wrath of Hera. But, instead of being burned to a crisp, she was turned into a cow. Although Zeus did this to hide her true identity, Hera was not fooled and demanded the cow as a gift. She

then sent the hundred-eyed monster Argos to guard it and keep Zeus from snatching it. Not satisfied with this punishment, she later sent a gadfly to torment the cow.

What do these stories tell us about the gods? They show that the ancients saw their deities as not much

Leto rests on her side with her babies, Apollo and Artemis.

different from humans, only more emotional, naughtier, and definitely more vengeful.

6 Arachne Spins Her Web

A spider's web is one of the wonders of nature. What can compare with its symmetry, its delicacy, its intricacy? The ancient Greeks immortalized one spider and her web in a myth that's beautiful … and horrifying.

Arachne Learns to Weave

Many centuries ago, there lived a beautiful young maiden named Arachne. Her father, Idmon, was a master dyer who trained Arachne from an early age as his helper. He had also instructed her in the art of weaving.

She mastered each skill quickly and soon was producing the finest work anyone had ever seen. But Arachne did not remain humble. "Certainly no god or goddess is better than I," she boasted. "Not even Athena, the goddess of weaving!"

Such a boast did not go unnoticed on Mount Olympus. Disguised as an old woman, Athena visited Arachne's hometown, where everyone was talking of the beautiful designs she wove on her loom. Athena approached Arachne while she was working. She said to Arachne, "Listen, mortals must not consider themselves better than the gods, who endow talents and skills."

Arachne was turned into a spider because of her hubris, or excessive pride.

Arachne ignored this warning, going so far as to say, "I challenge you to do better."

"I accept," Athena said as she revealed herself. Arachne began to tremble. But what could she do? She had to honor her word.

First, Arachne sat at the loom. She chose her theme: the misdeeds of the gods. She gradually regained her confidence ... even her haughtiness. Carefully and

Do you see the spider web pattern in this depiction of Arachne's weaving?

skillfully, she wove. At length she finished, certain that no one could surpass her masterpiece.

Athena Takes Her Turn

Athena took her place at the loom. As she wove, the divine fragrance of ambrosia and nectar filled the room. In the center of her piece were scenes of Mount Olympus and of Athena's founding of the city of Athens. In each corner, she depicted a mortal who had dared defy the gods.

"I was wrong," Arachne whispered.

Athena finished her masterpiece. The goddess touched Arachne with her magic spindle. As she did so, she said, "Live as an example of what happens to those who challenge the gods."

Arachne felt herself changing and wondered what happened. Soon she realized she had been transformed into a spider. Practicing the art for which she had been famous, Arachne spun.

So captivating was this story that Arachne's name became the Greek word for spider. In English, "arachnid" describes the group of invertebrates that includes spiders.

Lessons for Us All

Like Arachne's tale, Greek and Roman myths are full of lessons. These exciting stories tell of adventure. They also tell us about the values that ancient people held dear. Myths and legends show us how much the world has changed—and how much it has stayed the same!

Glossary

Amazons Members of a legendary race of female warriors who, the Greek believed, lived near the Black Sea.

city-state A city and its surrounding areas that has its own government and is an independent state, separate from neighboring countries or city-states.

custom A way of behaving that is widely accepted by a group of people; a tradition.

expeditions Journeys or trips.

famine A severe or extended lack of food.

immortal Living forever.

legends Traditional stories that may be thought of as historical or factual, but they cannot be proven.

myths Legends or stories that typically concern the origins of a people or explain natural or societal phenomena. Myths often include gods or supernatural beings.

oracle A priest or priestess who people believed spoke for the gods and could see the future.

phenomena Things that have been observed to happen, but that are sometimes hard to explain or understand; the plural of "phenomenon."

posse A group of people gathered for a common purpose.

quiver A container made to hold arrows.

Underworld The ancient Greek version of the afterlife, where souls go after a person dies.

vanquish Conquer.

Further Information

Books

Hamilton, Edith. *Mythology: Timeless Tales of Gods and Heroes*. New York: Grand Central Publishing, 2011.

Hunt, Jilly. *Roman Myths and Legends*. Oxford, UK: Raintree Press, 2013.

Napoli, Donna Jo. *Treasury of Greek Mythology*. Washington, DC: National Geographic Children's Books, 2011.

Websites

Ancient History Encyclopedia: Roman Mythology

http://www.ancient.eu/Roman_Mythology/

An overview of Roman (and Greek) mythology with some specific myths included.

Greek Mythology

https://www.greekmythology.com

A compendium of links to explore myths related to specific gods or specific stories in Greek myth.

National Geographic Kids: The Gods and Goddesses of Ancient Greece

https://www.natgeokids.com/za/discover/history/greece/greek-gods/

Learn more about the major figures of Greek mythology.

Project Gutenberg: E. M. Berens's *Myths and Legends of Ancient Greece and Rome*

https://www.gutenberg.org/files/22381/22381-h/22381-h.htm

An e-book on the myths of Ancient Greece and Rome for those that want to take a deeper look.

Index

Page numbers in **boldface** are illustrations.
Entries in **boldface** are glossary terms.